Innovate

Like Magic !

A proven, step-by-step process

For business innovation

Innovate Like Magic!

Innovate Like Magic!

Contents

Acknowledgments 5

Introduction 7

Chapter 1: Innovation Definition 15

Chapter 2: Why is Innovation Important? 19

Chapter 3: Barriers to Innovation 23

Chapter 4: The **CARPE NOVUM** Method 31

Chapter 5: **C**ulture of Curiosity 37

Chapter 6: **A**chievement Track Record 71

Chapter 7: **R**esearch Innovation Alternatives 79

Chapter 8: **P**roposal Generation 89

Chapter 9: **E**xecution - Launch into Delivery 97

Chapter 10: **N**avigate Obstacles 103

Chapter 11: **O**ffer Encouragement 109

Chapter 12: **V**ary the Plan 115

Chapter 13: **U**pdate Stakeholders 119

Chapter 14: **M**otivate for the Future 127

Chapter 15: Case Study - **Product** 133

Chapter 16: Case Study – **Process** 143

Chapter 17: Case Study – **Problem Solving** 153

Innovate Like Magic!

Chapter 18: Conclusion 165

Notes 167

About the Author 180

Acknowledgments

I wish to thank everyone who made this book possible....

- My wife, Bev, a major source of encouragement and steadfast support
- Family and friends, for their supportive relationships and advice
- My bosses over the years, for their support
- My teams for their amazing efforts
- My colleagues, from whom I learned a great deal by watching, questioning, and listening

I truly appreciate the help.

Innovate Like Magic!

Introduction

When I was 8 years old, I saw my very first magic show.

Early one Saturday morning, I was sitting cross-legged in front of our family's 13" Zenith black-and-white TV, waiting for Bugs Bunny and other cartoons. This was the typical fare on a Saturday morning back then.

On came *The Magic Land of AllaKazam*, the first weekly magic show made for television.

I had not seen a magic show before. Not many magicians traveled to the town of Stetsonville, population 319, in the central farmlands of Wisconsin. Magic on TV was not as commonplace as today, with shows like *America's Got Talent*, *Penn & Teller's Fool Us,* and David Blaine specials.

Innovate Like Magic!

Yet here was a 30-minute magic show specifically for kids, right in my living room!

I remember the scene like it was yesterday....

Mark Wilson, the magician on the show, began by showing a blank deck of playing cards while surrounded by kids my age. He fanned through the deck, from his left hand to his right, showing both sides of the blank cards as he fanned them. He then tapped on the deck with his finger while saying the magic word, "Allakazam!"

Innovate Like Magic!

In a waterfall of cards, the previously-blank deck had magically changed into a normal deck of cards, printed on both fronts and backs.

My eyes opened wide; my jaw dropped. Amazing!

How did he do it? He didn't switch the cards. He was surrounded by kids watching as intently as I was. There was no natural, rational explanation for what I just witnessed. I was in awe.

Secretly hoping one day I would learn how to change a blank deck of playing cards into a printed deck, how to make the impossible possible, I began my lifelong journey of curiosity and innovation.

Innovate Like Magic!

Innovation isn't magic, something that happens in a "ta-da" moment. It isn't something that happens to the creative few.

> "We do not need magic to transform our world. We carry all of the power we need inside ourselves already."[1]
>
> J.K. Rowling

I believe innovation can be created by anyone, in any company, with the help of a proven, step-by-step process for innovation. I call this process, CARPE NOVUM, Latin for "Seize Innovation" and have used it throughout my career.

While magicians do not share their secrets, in this book I will share the secrets of the CARPE NOVUM process for innovation. Here is quick overview of what lies ahead:

Chapter 1-3. Innovation Introduction

> What is the definition of innovation used in this book? Why is innovation important to business? What are common barriers to innovation? The first chapters answer those

questions and set the stage for defining the process to follow.

Chapter 4. The CARPE NOVUM Method

What are the steps in the CARPE NOVUM method? Here we outline the steps in the process. Each step is then detailed in subsequent chapters.

Chapter 5. Culture of Curiosity

How do you foster the culture needed for innovation? The first step is creating and encouraging a culture of curiosity. Curiosity leads to questions; questions lead to innovation.

Chapter 6. Achievement Track Record

Next comes having a track record of achievement, being able to deliver on current responsibilities. This gives confidence in your ability to deliver on an innovation opportunity.

Chapter 7. Research Innovation Alternatives

Where do innovation ideas come from? The third step is researching innovation

Innovate Like Magic!

alternatives, generating ideas, and selecting the best target(s) for innovation.

Chapter 8. Proposal Generation

Next is packaging the innovation effort, to present to senior executives for awareness and approval.

Chapter 9. Execution – Launch into Delivery

The fifth step addresses how to overcome fear and launch into delivery of the innovation.

Chapter 10. Navigate Obstacles

Innovation projects will encounter obstacles, often unexpected ones. Navigate around these obstacles to keep the project on track.

Chapter 11. Offer Encouragement

Participants in an innovation effort can become disheartened from experiencing dead ends or delays in delivering results.

Offering encouragement is essential to keep spirits up and to keep the innovation effort moving forward.

Chapter 12. Vary the Plan

Innovation efforts deal with the unknown, so it is unlikely that yours will be the perfect plan, requiring no modification. Vary the plan as needed. Iterate as needed.

Chapter 13. Update Stakeholders

Updating stakeholders as you go along is critically important. Keeping everyone in the loop helps sustain buy-in. Communicate, communicate, communicate.

Chapter 14. Motivate for the Future

The final step is motivating the team, the executives, and vendor partners for future innovation opportunities. Celebrate the effort, even if not successful. Learn and set the stage for future efforts.

Chapter 15-17. Innovation Case Studies

Here we apply the CARPE NOVUM method to three different case studies – one involving <u>product</u> innovation, the next a <u>process</u> innovation, and finally using innovation to solve a strategic business <u>problem</u>. Three different companies, with different appetites and needs for innovation, having successful innovation outcomes using the CARPE NOVUM method.

Let's begin with the definition of innovation....

Chapter 1: Innovation Definition

"A new idea, method, or device"

"The introduction of something new"[1]

Merriam-Webster.com

Let's begin with this very broad definition of innovation. Innovation is not the slight reworking of an old idea - it represents "the introduction of something new." We have many classic examples of innovation over the years, from the Edison light bulb to Marconi's radio to Steve Job's iPhone.

Innovate Like Magic!

And even more recently, during the global pandemic, we have also seen innovations appear:

- Drive-Through Testing, enabling patients to be tested for the virus without leaving their cars

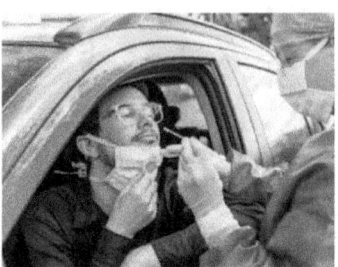

- Creating Personal Protective face shields using 3D printers

- Meetings via Zoom, adapting to work meetings and social gatherings via online video conferencing

I find that innovation is becoming an expectation of today's job, not only in Information Technology (IT), not only the responsibility of a select few "idea people" within an organization, but for everyone.

But how do you make innovation happen? We will explore in the following chapters how to seize this expectation and make innovation happen via a method I call, CARPE NOVUM (Latin for "seize innovation"). CARPE NOVUM will include how to find a target need or problem, how to identify an innovative solution, how to package it for action within a company, how to launch the innovation effort, and how to successfully manage such an effort.

But first, let's visit the question, why is innovation important?

Innovate Like Magic!

Chapter 2: Why is Innovation Important?

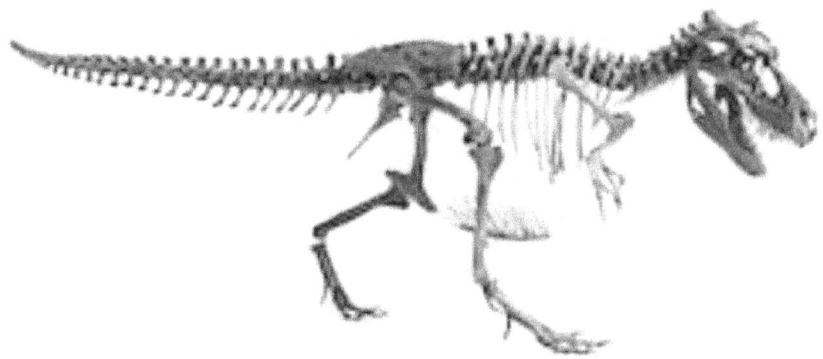

"If an established organization is not able to innovate, it faces decline and extinction."[1]

Peter Drucker, Management Expert

Drucker's words tell the story. Organizations no longer have the discretion to innovate - it is now a matter of survival. In IT, I have seen the Chief Information Officer (CIO) role evolve from merely keeping the systems running, to an expectation of innovation, transforming organizations with new digital solutions.

From an article by Amitabh Shukla, in Paggu.com,

Innovate Like Magic!

> "The importance of innovation is increasing and increasing significantly. In the current day economic scenario, innovativeness has become a major factor in influencing strategic planning. It has been acknowledged that innovation leads to wealth creation. Even though efficiency is essential for business success, in the long run, it cannot sustain business growth."[1]

Whether it means solving problems, adapting to technological change, seizing globalization opportunities, forging new ways of meeting customer expectations, or keeping up with the competition, innovation plays a vital role.

This importance is reflected in a Harris poll of 2,600 workers:

> "67% of workers say that generating new ideas is an important part of their job."[2]

Earlier in my career, I directed an R&D team within a Fortune 500 company. It was our mission to research new ideas for applicability within the enterprise. At that time, it was felt that employees were focused on their own responsibilities and did not have the time or skills to innovate, so innovation was centralized in my small, ten-person team. Clearly that mission has now been decentralized to all workers.

Post-pandemic, innovation will increase in importance. From the article, "COVID-19 Will Fuel the Next Wave of Innovation,"

> "...pandemics and recessions are accelerants to innovation... Over the longer term, Covid-19 has irrevocably changed the way businesses will compete over the next decade. Firms that choose to capitalize on these underlying changes will succeed and the ones that don't will get disrupted."[3]

But generating new ideas, even though important to the job, is not that simple, is it? Let's explore common barriers to innovation.

Innovate Like Magic!

Chapter 3: Barriers to Innovation

"If you don't know what your barriers are, it's impossible to figure out how to tear them down."[1]

John Manning

Typical barriers to innovation include limited staffing, limited budgets, resistance to change, having too much to do already, and not knowing how to innovate. Let's review each of these.

Innovate Like Magic!

- Limited Staffing

    "I don't have any staff to allocate to an innovation effort." The staff is already fully allocated to the existing workload. I sympathize. In my CIO role, I saw discretionary IT resources decline from 17% to zero, as the required workload increased year over year.

- Limited Budget

    Similarly, "My budget is already fully allocated for the year." We tend not to anticipate and budget for the unknown, so if an innovation opportunity arises during the year and requires funding, those funds may not be there or may need to come out of some other budget category.

- "We've always done it this way."

    This is the nemesis of innovation – being locked into old ways of doing things, being unwilling to change.

    I once worked on a project that called for a timing change in the daily bank deposit. The Finance Department clerk who made the deposit told me, "We always make our deposits at 2 p.m. We can't change that. That is a bank requirement." I then contacted the bank to ask if we could delay until 3 p.m. each day. "No problem!" was the bank's response, even though we had always done it at 2 p.m.

- Too Much to Do Already

    "In a recent survey by Accenture, more than 50% of respondents reported feeling too busy or too blocked at work to think up and propose new, innovative ideas...there's simply not any reserve energy left for strategic ideation."[2]

    Your plate may be already full. Being a CIO, for example, is a challenging job with broad demands and expectations. Whether the CIO's goal is to thrive, or merely to survive, you must balance:
    - Projects: delivering on time, on budget and with high quality
    - Costs: maintaining acceptable IT cost levels relative to overall business budgets

- Reliability: providing acceptable up time, response time and security of key systems
- Support: responding to customer and system needs for troubleshooting and preventive maintenance

These could be viewed as basic, traditional areas of responsibility, and they have been around since the beginning of IT.

Today, CIO demands and expectations include these four additional areas:
- Partnerships: building and managing relationships with technology vendors, business partners and executives within your company
- Staffing: providing the necessary resource levels and skill sets, including outsourcing
- Industry Comparisons: gathering intelligence on the competition and performing well relative to competitive benchmarks

- Innovation: using technology to bring new business solutions to the table

Some technology analysts have suggested there is too much for the CIO, that expectations are so high a CIO cannot possibly meet them. They further suggest the path for the CIO is to focus on one or two responsibilities, and do well at those. But can a CIO succeed or survive if projects are delivered well, but IT costs are out of control? Or what if costs are managed, but tech innovations are not introduced to the business? Or if innovation is brought forward, but vendor relationships are not cultivated?

Like juggling chainsaws, it is dangerous to take your eye off any of these.

From my book, *The Holistic CIO*,

> "I submit that a CIO must address all of these eight elements to be successful. He/she must be "holistic" in approach to the job and its underlying responsibilities."[3]

With all these expectations, you may already be exhausted....

What are you going to do with innovation?

- And one more barrier..."I don't know how to innovate." You may never have attempted this before. How do you begin? Where do you find innovative ideas? What process do you follow to make innovation happen?

In the following chapters we will review the process to overcome these barriers and make innovation happen.

The process enabled winning InformationWeek's top national award for Innovation in Data Analytics….

The Secret?

A hint: It did **not** require a big company, a big budget, a big staff, or ignoring your other responsibilities.

Innovate Like Magic!

Chapter 4: The CARPE NOVUM Method

"Plan the work, work the plan."[1]
Vince Lombardi

Latin for "Seize Innovation," CARPE NOVUM is a proven, how-to process I developed over decades of successful innovation efforts. It consists of

- 5 steps to plan and launch an innovation effort
- 5 more steps to help in accomplishing the innovation

Innovate Like Magic!

The first 5 steps, C-A-R-P-E, address researching and constructing the innovation plan:

1. **C**ulture of Curiosity

    The first step is creating and fostering a culture of curiosity. Curiosity leads to questions; questions lead to innovation.

2. **A**chievement

    Next comes having a track record of achievement, being able to deliver on current responsibilities. This gives confidence in your ability to deliver on an innovation opportunity.

3. **R**esearch

    Third is researching innovation alternatives, generating ideas, and selecting the best target for innovation.

4. **P**roposal

    Fourth is packaging the innovation effort, to present to senior executives for awareness and approval.

5. **E**xecution

    The fifth step is overcoming fear and launching into delivery of the innovation.

Innovate Like Magic!

With a plan built, the next 5 steps address accomplishing the plan, N-O-V-U-M:

6. **N**avigate Obstacles

    Innovation projects will encounter obstacles, often unexpected ones. Navigate around these obstacles to keep the project on track.

7. **O**ffer Encouragement

    Participants in an innovation effort can become disheartened, from experiencing dead ends or delays in delivering results. Offering encouragement is essential to keep spirits up.

8. **V**ary the Plan

Innovation efforts deal with the unknown, so it is unlikely that yours will be the perfect plan, requiring no modification. Vary the plan as needed.

9. **U**pdate

    Updating stakeholders as you go along is critically important. Keeping everyone in the loop helps sustain buy-in. Communicate, communicate, and communicate.

10. **M**otivate

    The final step, motivate the team, the executives, and vendor partners for future innovation opportunities. Celebrate the effort, even if not successful. Learn and set the stage for future efforts.

Innovate Like Magic!

Next: **C**ARPE NOVUM – Fostering a **Culture** of curiosity.

Chapter 5: Culture of Curiosity

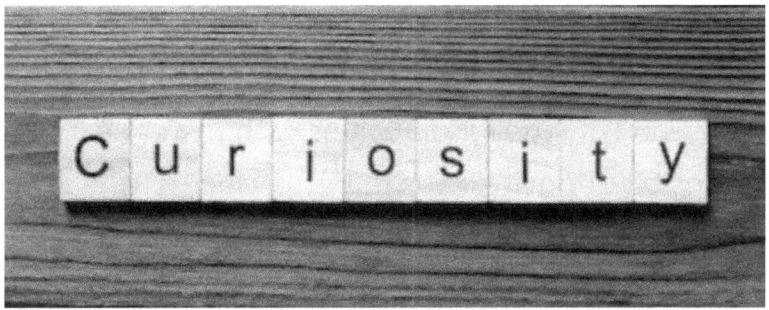

"I have no special talent. I am only passionately curious." [1]

Albert Einstein

Curiosity gets a bad rap. "Curiosity killed the cat." Curious George was always getting into trouble because of his curious nature. Opening Pandora's Box was not a good thing. We are taught from a young age that conformity is good, curiosity is not.

"Just do what I say." When you asked too many questions as a child, did your parents ever tell you that?

Innovate Like Magic!

> "Curiosity comes with questions and challenges the status quo; the answer is sure to originate innovation of some form."[2]
>
> Akila Balasubramaniyan,
>
> Harvard Business Review Group

A journey of innovation begins with fostering curiosity. Curiosity leads to better decisions, based on deep thought and creative solutions. It leads to deeper relationships with coworkers and vendor partners. It leads to <u>innovation</u> and better performance.

When asked what trait would most help leaders succeed, Dell's CEO Michael Dell responded, "I would put my bet on curiosity."[1]

Innovate Like Magic!

Curiosity Quiz

Are you curious? Let's take this short quiz and check….

1. **When I have an opportunity to learn a new skill, I**
   - _ A. Excitedly accept, as I like learning new things.
   - _ B. Decline, as I already know what I need.
   - _ C. Decline, as it feels like too much extra work.
2. **When I am in a meeting, I**
   - _ A. Talk as much as possible to share my ideas.
   - _ B. Talk sometimes and listen sometimes.
   - _ C. Mostly listen to learn what others say.
3. **When someone comes in to ask for help with a problem, I**
   - _ A. Quickly tell them how to solve the problem.
   - _ B. Ask them how they would solve the problem.
   - _ C. Decline, since I have enough problems.
4. **When assigned to a project team, I**
   - _ A. Immediately take the lead and direct others.
   - _ B. Ignore what others say as I have better ideas.
   - _ C. Listen to what others say, add my ideas, and ask questions. Everyone works together.

Innovate Like Magic!

If you answered,

1. A
2. C
3. B
4. C

you are well on your way to fostering curiosity. More such questions can be found at

https://instituteofcuriosity.survey.fm/curiosity-test?p=1 [3]

Following are some specific suggestions on developing or nurturing a culture of curiosity:

- In yourself
- With your staff
- With in-house business partnerships
- With vendor partners
- With ideas
- With projects
- With learning

- **Fostering Curiosity in Self**

    o **Ask Questions**

    "A lot of bad leadership comes from an inability or unwillingness to ask questions. What they don't realize is the dumbest question can be very powerful."[4]

    Michael Parker,
CEO, Dow Chemical

    You may feel uncomfortable or shy about asking questions. You may want to avoid looking dumb in front of others. Ask anyway.

Innovate Like Magic!

My first job after college, as a computer programmer for a Midwest life insurance company, taught me a great lesson about asking questions.

After eagerly completing programmer training at the company, I drew my first real assignment – producing letters to dividend policyholders. This entailed

- Identifying customers with the appropriate policy plan identifier
- Calculating the dividend, with specifications provided by the actuarial department
- Printing a nicely-formatted letter, informing the policyholder of the precise amount he/she was being paid

I carefully listened to instructions from my supervisor. I followed the instructions precisely. The program selected the dividend-paying policies, calculated the correct amount of the dividend for each policyholder, and produced the letter for mailing. The program looked good. The letters were printed and mailed out.

Within a few days, the phone calls began. "My husband died three years ago. Is this some kind of sick joke?" asked one upset widow. The letters had been sent to <u>dead people</u> as well as living policyholders. I didn't know both active and inactive policies were on the same master file. I wasn't told; I didn't ask.

My first assignment was a disaster! I didn't sleep that night, convinced I would be fired for causing this, and fearful that my IT career might be over before it had even started. But three good things happened:

1. I wasn't fired. The company was very forgiving.
2. Phone calls were made to the households incorrectly selected, apologizing for the error. Generally, they too were very forgiving.
3. I asked questions on my next assignment, and ever since!

A painful lesson indeed, but my career benefited greatly from the experience.

Innovate Like Magic!

Just after writing about my letters to dead people, a disaster thought to be unique, I read the following:

> "Many Americans are eagerly anticipating stimulus checks of up to $1,200 starting this week, but in a few cases the recipients won't be celebrating — because they're dead. The IRS began distributing $290 billion in direct cash payments within the past week as part of a $2 trillion CARES Act stimulus bill, and anecdotes are already surfacing about the IRS issuing money to the deceased."[5]

Unfortunately, this was not as unique as I had thought.

- **Listen**

    Most of us focus on being understood. While others are talking, we might be quietly formulating our response. And we may even assume what the person is about to say, without listening intently.

    "If I were to summarize in one sentence the single most important principle I have learned in the field of interpersonal relationships, it would be this: Seek first to understand, then to be understood."[6]

Dr. Stephen R. Covey

Listen to others to fully understand. Be curious about what others are saying from their perspectives and experiences. Take in this valuable input before responding.

- **Read**

    When given a new role in the organization, managing a call center, I read as much as I could to prepare. What are typical issues in a call center and how do others address them? What are best-in-class stats for answering calls? And so on. Reading provided the answers for me.

    Having this added knowledge, this rich frame of reference, I was better prepared to lead the new team. And I would follow this pattern with every new assignment — read as much as possible early on to help assess where we were and to help formulate a plan forward.

Innovate Like Magic!

Read not only about your field, but be curious about topics outside your field as well. The broad perspective will enable you to offer ideas from this expanded base of knowledge.

- **Fostering Curiosity in Staff**

- ○ **Encourage questions**

    Demonstrate that it is ok for others to ask questions of you. You may feel you already do this, but in a survey of 3,000 employees from a cross-section of industries, "70% said they face barriers to asking more questions at work. " [7]

    Employees may be fearful of bothering you, or appearing incompetent, or being difficult. Or you may be subconsciously or inadvertently shutting down questions. Maybe you are concerned the questions are wasting time, when you are concerned about deadlines.

When there are tight deadlines, are you providing time for questions that might lead to a better direction or result? You may be taking the questions as a challenge to your authority, but try to look beyond that to the value within the questions. More information can lead you to better decisions.

- **Empowerment**

    Another deterrent to curiosity in staff is micromanagement. Constant, tight oversight may cause the employee to disengage and to lose interest.

    For example, my predecessor in managing the call center had implemented a cost-control procedure that all spending by the staff required her signoff. This created frustration and delay in solving the customer's problem, in a team that already faced high stress and high turnover levels.

I empowered the call center representatives to use their discretion in spending money to solve a customer's problem, up to a set amount. This empowered them to solve the problem and make it happen in real time, without the extra step of checking with the manager. (Side benefit: it also lightened my workload of such requests.)

- **Lead by Example**

    In my first 60 days as a CIO, my focus was formulating a plan for IT, one tailored to the specific needs of this organization. I had seen other CIOs fail by rigidly following the plans of their prior company, without adapting those plans to the culture, the technology, or the needs of the current company.

    So how did I go about learning about the organization and formulating an appropriate plan? In those first 60 days, I met individually with each member of the IT team. Yes, this filled up my schedule. My message was four-fold: a thank-you, sharing my plan to develop an IT plan, asking them a question, and asking if they had questions for me.

First I thanked them for their service to the organization. By the surprised looks I received, it was clear to me they had not heard "thank you" often. There was one element of my plan already.

Next I clarified that I would not instantly produce a plan, but instead would meet with each team member, collect information first, and then formulate a plan within 60 days.

They knew the organization better. I was an outsider. So I asked each person, "What can I do to make IT better?" And I listened. And I asked clarifying questions.

The most common response - communication within IT, making sure the right hand knew what the left hand was doing. Communication had not happened consistently in the past, and was an irritant to many. The resulting plan reflected this input, emphasizing communication both internally and to our customers, with no surprises.

We reinforced this with the introduction of a project methodology, which included a communication plan to all stakeholders both inside and outside of IT. In our monthly "all-hands" staff meetings, we also shared project plans and status. No surprises.

I concluded each one-on-one meeting by asking if they had any questions for me. The questions tended to be about their training and personal development, so I recognized another important element to the plan.

- **Hire curious people**

    In a study across 10 organizations by INSEAD's Spencer Harrison, "The results showed that the most curious employees sought the most information from coworkers, and the information helped them in their jobs – for instance, it boosted their creativity in addressing customer concerns." [7]

How do you identify curious applicants? Ask about past projects, problems they have solved and how, interests outside of work, or books they are reading. Look for signs of personal growth and a curious mind.

And the questions they ask may be more indicative of curiosity than the answers they provide. Do they ask questions? Are they thought-provoking, deep questions about the organization? Do they ask questions outside the role they for which they are applying?

> "We run this company on questions, not answers."[8]
>
> Eric Schmidt, Google's former CEO

You may even consider allocating staff time for curiosity and innovation. Google is known for allocating 20% of an employee's time to anything they desire. 3M had 15%, which led to the Post-It note. [9]

One of my best hires over the years was not the usual applicant with programming experience. She was smart, asked questions, and had business experience. I was confident she could be taught the necessary technical skills. For me this was a bold hire, hiring for curiosity and diversity of experience. Not only did she do well within my team and within the company, but went on to become CEO at another company.

- **Reinforce/Reward Curiosity**

    Consider opportunities to thank individuals demonstrating this behavior. Maybe thank the individual in person? Or send a personal handwritten note? Or recognize the person in a team meeting? This type of recognition encourages such behavior in the future – more curiosity, more questions, and more innovative ideas. And it works not only with the person but with the whole team.

    At the encouragement of a colleague, I tried attaching a stick-on gold star to a good idea submitted by a member of my team. I doubted that such childish recognition would be a motivator to a professional. To my surprise, the person was thrilled. The team would have killed for those gold stars. The reward can be something seemingly trivial, and can indeed motivate a highly-paid professional staff.

- **Fostering Curiosity with Business Partnerships**

Questions can lead to a closer relationship with internal business partners. I tried to have coffee with our business executives periodically to share what IT was working on, but more importantly to ask questions. How is IT doing, in your view? What could we improve? What problems keep you up at night? What might we do to help you with those problems? These questions can lead to better collaboration and planning.

One day I had to deliver bad news to one of these business executives – the system was down, we had our best people working on it, and recovery was estimated at two hours. I had delivered such messages in the past, and was anticipating the typical lecture about the impact of such an outage on the business and on their goals.

The reply this time was different this time, "What can we do to help?" This shocking response was the result of having built a solid partnership through periodic meetings and asking questions.

- **Fostering Curiosity with Vendor Partners**

Similarly asking questions can form a closer bond with your vendor partners.

Do you share your strategic business plan with your vendor partners? I provided a one-page condensed version of the business plan to share with vendors, both existing and new. Vendors liked this as it was a faster way to learn this information, much faster than their typical 30-minute needs-analysis meeting.

Then I would ask, "How can you help me achieve these goals?" They may be able to bring current and future products, industry insight, or how other clients have addressed such needs.

Innovate Like Magic!

Questions can also lead to better contracts. By learning about the vendor, you can learn key terms that are nonnegotiable and terms that are. You may learn about critical timeframes for the vendor, to increase your leverage. Using this insight, you may come away with a significantly better price.

My employer at the time, a mid-sized health insurance company, produced large volumes of paper – letters, Explanation of Benefits, and checks. This print workload was outsourced to a local vendor. I became manager of the data center, which included responsibility for the contract as it came up for renewal.

My curiosity led to questions of their capability; a site visit confirmed they had the equipment and staff to deliver. I asked my staff about their track record. In reviewing the logs, the vendor had been late a couple of times, but never failed to deliver. I interviewed the business units and they were satisfied with the vendor's service. All looked promising for a renewal.

I asked one more question of the vendor, "How do I know your price is fair?" I was new to the role and honestly did not know the answer without going out for competitive bids.

The price dropped one million dollars a year, on the spot. One question, one million dollars, instantly!

We were a major customer and the vendor could not afford to lose our business. The price drop was to discourage competitive bidding. That made me even more curious, so we did go out to bid and found that our current vendor was now competitive. That plus their track record earned them the renewal.

- **Fostering Curiosity with Ideas**

Who invented the digital watch? You may be surprised to learn that the digital watch was invented by the Swiss. But they saw this new idea as merely a novelty. Real watches were mechanical, like those the Swiss had made for generations. They continued to make mechanical watches.

The Japanese, however, took the idea of digital watches and ran with it, becoming dominant in the watch market.

The moral: be open to new, disruptive ideas (or risk losing your market like the Swiss). Watch (pun intended) out for locking in on an idea because "we have always done it this way."

In another example, Henry Ford succeeded initially with the Ford model T, but he remained fixated on that model.

"Competitors such as General Motors started producing an array of models and soon captured the main share of the market." "Ford stopped experimenting and innovating and fell behind."[7]

Be open to new ideas, to new ways of doing things. Beware the trap of "we have always done it this way."

- **Fostering Curiosity with Projects**

- o **NASA**

    In the early days of NASA, according to an urban myth, astronauts discovered that ballpoint pens would not work properly in zero gravity. NASA scientists spent millions of dollars to solve the problem, eventually coming up with a pen that writes in zero gravity and at any angle. The Russians used a pencil. [10]

    While the NASA story above may not be factual, it does make a point about pursuing overly-complex solutions, wasting time and money. Your staff may want to generate just such a solution. Always look for simplicity.

A manager in one of our business departments requested this of me - faster printing, to save time for his staff doing high volume printing. Here is the conversation.

- "Why do you print these documents?" I asked.
- "To prove we have thoroughly tested changes for the upcoming upgrade."
- "Who do you need to prove it to?" I asked.
- "IT" was the response.
- "I'm IT, and I trust you are doing the testing you say you are."

While we could have engineered a technology solution for faster printing, it would have been unnecessary. No printing was needed at all ... a Russian pencil.

- **Diversify the Team**

    Add diversity of ideas, perspectives, and backgrounds to a project team. Bringing different strengths and fresh eyes to the project can lead to more options and more effective results.

    > "Synergy means the whole is greater than the sum of its parts ... 1+1=3"[11]
    >
    > Stephen Covey

    Or, as a former boss once bluntly told me, "If you and I agree on everything, one of us is unnecessary."

- **Allow Time for Ideas**

    A common challenge with projects is an aggressive timetable. Too often the timeframe is so tight that the team does not have time to come up with multiple approaches. It is forced to go with the first idea, the easy idea, in order to meet the timeline. Try to provide enough time for curiosity and multiple approaches to be considered.

Innovate Like Magic!

- **Keep Asking, "Is There is a Better Way?"**

    As manager of a PC support team years ago, I inherited a process that provided the installation of 30 PCs per month, with each PC being a custom build. We needed a better way in order to meet increasing demand.

    The team and I revamped the process, implementing standard configurations and simplifying testing. Rather than having the PC team test the PC configuration, then the Network team test network connectivity, and then the Application team test the apps, one person did it all in one stop. And the tester left a personal note for the user confirming all had been tested.

    We were then able to reduce the cost per PC installation from $65 to $24 with the new process. And we were able to install 130 PCs per month (versus 30) without increasing staff, an efficiency increase of over 300%!

- **Fostering Curiosity with Learning**

Grow the talents of your staff by providing opportunities to acquire the skills and experiences needed for diverse thinking and innovation.

- **Fight for your Training Budget**

    When budget-cutting, it may be easy to cut training dollars, but such a move will not help the innovation challenge. I opted for low-cost, local training and web-based training to spread the training budget as far as possible.

    And when there is no budget? Look for and negotiate speaking engagements that will cover the conference fee and travel. If a vendor conference, offer to speak about your success using the vendor's product or service. Combine potential conferences with other business travel to help cut costs. Be creative.

- **Provide Opportunities for Cross-Training**
  This adds depth to your overall team and enriches the knowledge base of the individuals. For example, PC support team members may want to grow their network support skills. Rather than having them wait for an opening on the network team or leaving the company to find these skills, provide lunch-and-learn sessions or internships on the network team.

- **Share Knowledge Within the Team**
  When staff leaves, they may take institutional knowledge with them, knowledge gained through years of hands-on experience at your company. Try to capture this knowledge so it does not leave with the person. For example,

Innovate Like Magic!

we built an in-house wiki to store and share those nuggets of how-to information within the team.

- **Build a "Hostage Exchange" Program**
  Imagine an exchange of individuals on a bridge in the morning fog....

I applied this swap idea within the company. A business user joins the IT team for a limited amount of time, such as six weeks, to learn about our processes and challenges. He/she is assured of going back to the business team when the assignment is completed. In return, an IT person temporarily joins the business team to learn of their processes and challenges.

This is an investment in two people, a broadening experience for both. I have learned that it also creates long-term allies within each group. [9]

- **Venture Outside your Industry**

    While there is plenty of information within your industry or specialty, there are valuable ideas outside as well. Take in a broad range of topics. For example, I tried to attend one conference per year outside the healthcare industry.

    James Dyson, inventor of the bagless vacuum cleaner, used an outside idea to create his famous invention. Said Dyson, "Then one day I was at a local sawmill and noticed how the sawdust was being removed from the air by large industrial cyclones. My engineering instinct kicked in. Could that work on a smaller scale?"[12]

To begin your innovation journey, foster a <u>culture</u> of curiosity. Curiosity leads to questions; questions lead to innovation.

Innovate Like Magic!

Next: CARPE NOVUM – Building a track record of **Achievement**.

Chapter 6: Achievement Track Record

"Business will not accept innovation from a low-performing IT organization." [1]

Larry Wolff, President and COO,

Ouellette & Associates Consulting

And I suspect that observation about IT would apply to any department or individual within an organization.

Innovate Like Magic!

- **Basic Responsibilities**

    By delivering on your basic responsibilities, such as maintaining costs or completing projects, you establish credibility with your business peers and senior leadership. If you have a track record of successful delivery, you are more likely to be trusted on an innovation effort.

- **Third-Party Measures**

    By using third-party measures, you can present a credible story of how well you and your department are doing. Often, your peers and senior leadership are not aware of such benchmarks or competitive intelligence, so this provides valuable context for your progress reports.

    As CIO, I learned from industry analysts that best-in-class system uptime for a healthcare organization with an Electronic Health Record (HER) system was 99.8%. We had 99.96% or better for 4 consecutive years. This clearly communicated our achievement in a basic responsibility.

- **Gathering Comparisons**

    How do you gather such measures and comparisons?

    - **Join Local and National Groups**

        Associations, like the Society for Information Management (SIM), provide excellent networking opportunities. Such networking can provide insights, ideas, strategies, vendor evaluations and much more. Leverage such opportunities to gather competitive benchmarks and knowledge about your competitors.

    - **Local Peer Groups**

        If this does not exist in your area, consider initiating one. These discussions provide insights into such topics as budgets, plans, staffing or outages. Such information can provide excellent competitive intelligence. For example, did a competitor suffer a significant outage, while your IT stats showed best-in-class uptime?

Innovate Like Magic!

- **Vendor's User Group**

  Through user groups, you can glean common practices among customers of that vendor. For example, staffing levels for support or per cent of budget allocated. Are you spending too much or too little in comparison? What has been the experience with implementing the vendor's latest release?

- **Attend Local and National Conferences**

  Include conferences not only within your industry, but outside as well.

  - **Inside your industry**

    This not only provides topics of interest to the industry in general, but on several occasions our competitors gave presentations. Usually secretive, the competitor openly outlined their strategies, projects, successes and challenges. Take good notes!

  - **Outside your industry**

While industry events provide insights into your industry and competitors, sometime the best ideas or best practices come from outside your industry. Best in class may be far better than best in your industry. Be open to attending occasional events outside your industry as well. I tried to attend one or two such events per year for perspective.

- Work with Vendor Partners
  - **Existing Vendors**

    They may be able to provide advance notice of products or features in their pipeline, possibly under non-disclosure agreements. Explore if you, as a valued customer, might have a window into their innovation. They may also share the contact information of customers who are early adopters, another source of information on forthcoming products and early experiences.

- **New Vendors**

  These, too, may also provide insight into the industry and who is doing what. While not your vendor, this may be an existing vendor for your competitor. The vendor may have competitive knowledge and may share what is being worked on in the industry and with competitors.

- **Read and Research**

  Competitors may publish articles or be quoted in magazines. I would review technology magazines (e.g., Computerworld, InformationWeek, CIO magazine) and industry magazines (e.g., Healthcare IT News).

  Search online sources for industry themes, your competitors or even individuals. For example, a megasearch engine like www.dogpile.com (I did not name it) searches the web using multiple search engines.

Take surveys, like the SIM IT Trends Survey or vendor-specific surveys, so you can learn about and use the results for competitive insights.

- **Industry Analysts**

    Analysts like Gartner and IDC are good sources for IT industry benchmarks, like uptime in healthcare or IT budget as a percent of revenue. You may have similar sources.

    For example, we learned from an analyst that we had already achieved best-in-class uptime in the healthcare industry. Couple that with known outages for our competitors, and we had a complete story to share for credibility with the board.

- **Ask Your Competitors**

    If you are struggling to find competitive data, you can also try asking. For example, say "I'm

Innovate Like Magic!

struggling with maintenance costs. Are you experiencing that?" Your competitors may or may not respond, but you won't know unless you ask.

If you have a track record of successful delivery, your peers and senior leadership are more likely to trust you in delivering an innovation.

To paraphrase what Marie Kondo might say, "Let your achievements spark joy!"[2]

Deliver on your core responsibilities, building a track record of <u>achievement</u>. This gives confidence in your ability to deliver on an innovation opportunity.

Next: CARPE NOVUM – **Researching** innovation alternatives.

Chapter 7: Research Innovation Alternatives

"The best way to have a good idea is to have lots of ideas."[1]

Dr. Linus Pauling,

Nobel Prize winner in chemistry

First align with business needs. Then follow Pauling's advice to generate as many ideas as possible, from the sources that follow, to meet those needs.

- **Alignment**
    Align your innovation effort with key business needs.
    - ○ **Strategic Business Plan**
        Read your organization's strategic plan to learn key directional statements. Organizations typically are focused on operational excellence, product leadership, or customer intimacy, as defined in the book, *The Discipline of Market Leaders*:

        "By operational excellence, we mean providing customers with reliable products and services at competitive prices, delivered with minimal difficulty or inconvenience. By product leadership, we mean providing products that continually redefine the state of the art. And by customer intimacy, we mean selling the customer a total solution, not just a product or service."[2]

        Align with the strategic direction of the organization, to contribute to the success of the plan and to garner support for your innovation effort.

- o **Collaborate with Business Execs**

    Learn their pain points, again to contribute to organizational needs and also to gain support for your innovation direction.

- **Sources of Ideas**

    Where do ideas come from? Leave no stone unturned in seeking alternatives.

    - o **Your Ideas and Experience**

        Draw from your own past - companies, projects, training, and experience.

        Some may not think they are creative enough to come up with innovation, that this is the job of some other person or department. But you have a wealth of experience and training. Bring this to the table, as only you can. It is OK to steal (or reuse) ideas from your past.

I once proposed an innovative marketing idea in a former company, but that company was focused on cost containment and my idea was focused on growth. The idea went nowhere. While working for a growth-oriented company years later, I dusted off the idea and it was enthusiastically implemented. Draw from your experience.

- **Draw from your Team**
    Just as you have a wealth of experience to draw upon, so does your staff. Think of all the companies they have collectively worked for and the diversity of their backgrounds. Tap into this resource. It may be as simple as asking them for ideas in a group discussion about the strategic plan.

- **Consult with your Vendor Partners**
    Share your strategic plan with your key vendor partners, to the extent

possible without violating confidentiality or competitive secrecy. I condense key points into a one-page summary. How can they help if they don't know where you and your company are headed? Draw from their experience with other clients facing similar challenges.

Ask about the vendor's product or technology pipeline. An innovative solution may be forthcoming that you were not aware of. You may need to sign a nondisclosure agreement to obtain this information, but better to be prepared than surprised.

- **Draw from Industry Analysts**

    Consult with industry analysts like Gartner, IDC, and Forrester. I tried to sync with the analysts as least annually to be sure I was aligned with current technology trends and direction. In those trends may also be innovative products or ideas. Even if the products are not immediately available, knowledge can help you position for them.

- **Network with Your Peers**

    Look for, or initiate, networking opportunities with peers both inside and outside your industry. A great example is the Society for Information Management (SIM). The solutions you seek may already have been implemented in another company or industry.

- **Attend Conferences**

    Consider conferences both inside and outside your industry. These provide topics and discussions of interest, plus provide networking opportunities with attendees. Conferences also provide access to peers outside of your geographic area, broadening your reach for ideas.

- **Customer Surveys and Focus Groups**

    Ask your customers for ideas and feedback. Once when considering the innovative idea of data sharing between healthcare organizations, we held focus groups to learn their reactions. Rather than hearing data privacy concerns, instead we heard from customers that they not only supported the idea, but thought we were doing it already.

- **Data Analytics**

    As you will see in the Case Study on Problem Solving, look to the data collected within your organization for ideas, findings, trends, and guidance. As a former boss said occasionally, "Let's not confuse things with the facts." Data analytics can provide the facts to guide you.

- **Crowdsourcing**

    A relatively new approach, utilize the ideas and solutions from an even broader group through crowdsourcing. Often by tapping into social media or crowdsourcing sites like Kickstarter (www.kickstarter.com) and 99Designs (www.99designs.com), you have access to people with skill sets not available within your company. Another option to consider, crowdsourcing can be valuable to projects and problem solving.

- **Prioritization**

    In case there are too many good ideas on your list, you may need a prioritization step. In IT, there are typically more projects than resources (e.g., people, money) to do them. So we prioritize. In case we cannot complete all projects, at least the most important ones are been addressed.

    > "Innovation is not about saying yes to everything. It is about saying no to all but the most crucial."[3]
    >
    > Steve Jobs

    Consider, for example, graphing your ideas on a simple grid where the Y axis represents the level of alignment and benefit associated with the idea and the X axis represents the effort or risk.

Innovate Like Magic!

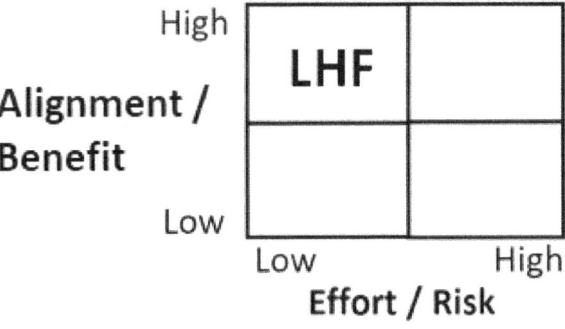

Choose ideas in the high alignment/benefit and low effort/risk quadrant, above labeled LHF for "Low-Hanging Fruit." This quadrant is advantageous over ideas in the low fulfillment and high effort/risk quadrant. If only some ideas can be pursued because of staffing or funding limitations, let it be those ideas in the upper left quadrant.

Research your innovation options. Align with the strategic business plan, generate ideas tapping as many sources as possible, and select the best target(s) via prioritization.

Next: CARPE NOVUM – generating a **Proposal**.

Innovate Like Magic!

Chapter 8: Proposal Generation

"Qualifying an opportunity at the outset helps you determine whether it's worth pursuing at all, and, if it is, with how much effort."[1]

Tom Sant

With the innovation idea selected, how do you package this for approval within your organization? The key elements are alignment, benefits, resources, risks, and a call to action. This can be as brief as one page, as brevity is desirable for any executive presentations, but the proposal needs to address each of these elements.

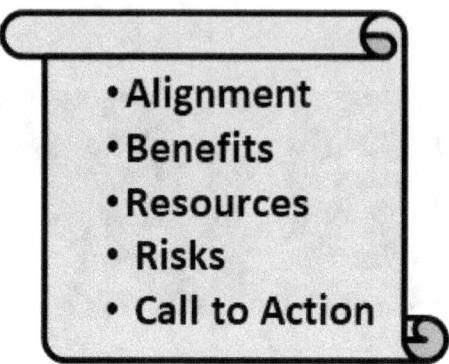

- **Alignment**

    With other projects competing for limited staff and funding, show that your proposal is aligned with the strategic plan of the organization. This will improve your chances of approval, as senior leadership will give priority to those efforts that work toward fulfillment of the strategic plan.

    I once proposed a cross-selling project, called "No Member Left Behind," aimed at increasing the growth of our health insurance company. Group insurance and individual insurance were two separate, almost competitive, profit centers within the company. As a policyholder was terminated from a group plan, for example to become an entrepreneur, I suggested we implement a cross-selling process to retain that member, reaching out in a mailing to offer our individual insurance. The person knows our company, and we know the person. Using the group policy information to provide a pre-filled, easy application for individual insurance, the idea prevents the individual from needing to shop for new insurance.

The idea was quickly rejected, not because it was a bad idea, but because the company was laser-focused on cost saving. If the project didn't quickly save money, it was not approved. My proposal was not aligned with the business plan.

Several years later, at a different health insurance company, I resurrected that same idea. This company was focused on growth and so was my proposal. It was enthusiastically approved and implemented. The VP of Individual Sales said, "I believe you have identified a huge opportunity for individual business."

The same innovative idea, aligned in one company and not aligned in another, provided me an important a lesson on the importance of this aspect of the proposal.

- **Benefits**

    In this section of the proposal, speak to how and how much the organization would be rewarded by moving forward. This may be in the form of Return on Investment (ROI), which is common, but ROI may not be the primary benefit. Perhaps this idea will have an impact on market share or on improved quality of healthcare services provided, for example.

    Because this is an innovation project and the exact benefits may be unknown, try to provide your best estimate or range for the benefit. In the case of ROI, this is like a reverse of the Price Is Right. You want to your estimate to be close to, but over the ROI necessary for approval. But not so far over that you lose credibility.

    In proposing to build an innovative Large Case Management system for our company, the first of its kind in the industry, I estimated an annual cost savings of $250,000, which was significant enough to achieve approval. In the first year, the system saved $4 million! No one, including me, would have believed a $4 million ROI estimate upfront.

- **Resources**

    What staffing and funding is needed to pursue this innovation project? This represents the time and money not being allocated to other organizational needs, and should be spelled out here.

- **Risks**

    Innovation projects rarely come with a guarantee. Set expectations by identifying the risks involved. I use the following chart to illustrate that early in the curve, in the pioneering phase, risks of failure are higher. Risks of additional costs are also higher as it will take longer and more money to resolve problems than with a mature, proven solution.

Innovate Like Magic!

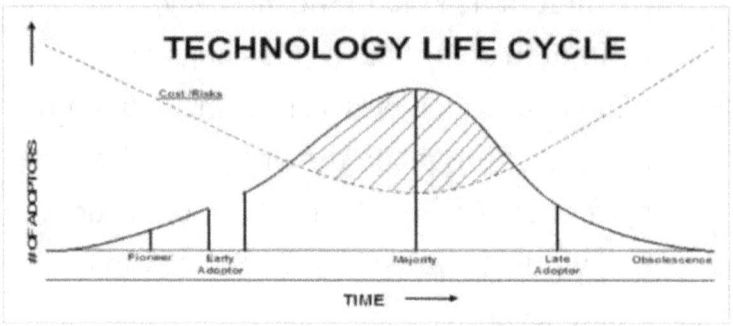

The diagram is my adaptation of the work of Geoffrey Moore in his book, *Crossing the Chasm.*[2] It takes his bell curve of the various stages of a technology product's evolution and adds my inverse, dotted line representing cost and risks.

If you are using a mature technology with high adoption, costs and risks will tend to be low. If you are looking to save IT budget money, this is the place you would want to be. For example, this is the place we wanted to be with our infrastructure — low cost and reliable.

Using a technology nearing obsolescence similarly brings higher costs, usually in the form of higher maintenance and the risks of the vendor sun-setting the product.

This curve applies not only to technology, but to cars, breakfast cereal, and more.

- **Call to Action**

    Having addressed alignment, benefits, resources, and risks, close the proposal with a specific call for approval to proceed.

Additional tips for making this document executive-friendly can be found in the upcoming chapter, Updating Stakeholders.

Package the innovation effort to present to senior executives for awareness and approval. Your Proposal should show alignment with the strategic business plan, benefits to the organization, resources needed, potential risks, and a call to action.

Next: CARPE NOVUM - **Execution** of the innovation plan.

Innovate Like Magic!

Chapter 9: Execution - Launch into Delivery

"You can't plow a field simply by turning it over in your mind."[1]

Gordon B. Hinckley

You have completed the proposal, and it has been accepted. Congratulations! You have prepared. You are ready. Now is the time to put your proposal into action.

- **Fear**

    With approval of the innovation proposal, fear and procrastination may hamper your response. You may be thinking:

    - Can we actually deliver on this new project?

    - Can we meet the deadlines?

    - What about all our other projects?

    These questions may hamper your response.

    Sir Richard Branson advises, "Don't let fear hold you back from achieving your full potential. Harness it and channel it into passion. Everything you've ever wanted is on the other side of fear."[2]

    This is your opportunity. I suspect many of us, if asked, would say we want to make a difference, to have an impact on the organization. Innovation efforts can make such a difference in product, service, cost, growth and more. Launch into this next step - project delivery.

- **Project Management**

Innovate Like Magic!

Establish or foster the use of a project management methodology. This adds consistency to how projects are executed, tracked and reported. Projects are difficult; a methodology will help your odds of success.

If your organization has a traditional or agile project management methodology, consider staying with that. But innovation efforts are often smaller in scope, with a shorter timeline. This type of project may be more appropriate for a light project management methodology. In my experience, a full project management methodology may be too much. Ends and means can become confused, with an emphasis on completing the PM forms and not on delivering results.

- PM-EZ

    The typical project management methodology, defined in several thick binders, may be too heavy for an innovation project. Something lighter was called for, to enable more focus on results rather than administrative overhead.

Innovate Like Magic!

We overcame this obstacle by developing PM-EZ (like a 1040-EZ short form), a lightweight project management methodology where each step could be as brief as one page. If you are not sending astronauts into space, you may consider using the following lightweight project management methodology, which I call PM-EZ.[3]

- **The Project Charter**, like an overall statement of work, defines the project objective, key roles and responsibilities, milestones, communication approach (e.g., status reporting), overall schedule and costs. This document defines the game plan.

- **The Project Change Request** is the vehicle for changes in deliverables or time frames, with acknowledgement of the impact of those changes. With appropriate signoff, this form makes those changes official. If you are developing in iterations, this would be the place to record and accommodate those iterations.

- **The Status Report** gathers status information on a regular schedule (weekly, monthly, etc.) on project costs, timing and milestones, and presents it in an executive-friendly red/yellow/green (danger/caution/ok) format. Where something is red or yellow, state briefly the actions you are taking to make the element green. This demonstrates that you are watching the total project, are taking corrective action where needed, and will report again on the defined schedule.

- **The Issue Log** tracks the various challenges that arise, who is assigned responsibility for resolution, and the final outcome. This is helpful in assuring that each issue is addressed, and helpful in the Lessons Learned meeting at the end of the project.

- **The Project Closure and Signoff** recaps the charter and results, and looks for sponsor sign-off that the project has met expectations.

- **The Lessons-Learned Meeting** recaps the project journey — what went well, what did not go well. How can the methodology be improved for the next project? Continuous improvement is the goal.

Overcome fear and launch into the execution of the innovation effort using project management, like PM-EZ.

Next: CARPE **NOVUM** - **Navigating** obstacles.

Chapter 10: Navigate Obstacles

"The best laid schemes o'mice an' men

gang aft agley."[1]

Robert Burns

Because innovation projects deal with so many unknowns, obstacles are likely to crop up. Here are some typical obstacles, a general approach to overcoming them, and a couple of examples.

- **Lack of Communication**

    According to a Project Management Institute survey, almost one-third of all project failures are caused by poor communication. [2]

    Status updates may not have occurred when needed, or the right stakeholders may not have been informed.

    A communication plan is included in project management, like PM-EZ, for this reason. Anticipate what needs to be shared via status updates, and deliver them regularly. Anticipate who needs these communications and be sure these stakeholders receive the updates.

    When interviewing a project manager (PM) candidate, I asked, "What do you see as the top 3 things a PM should do to be successful?" The answer, "Communicate, communicate, and communicate." She was quickly hired.

- **Lack of Project Management**

    While it may be tempting to attack innovation without a plan, like Nike's Just Do It campaign, project management brings a needed discipline to the project. I have experienced that PM improves your odds of success, and avoids reliance on individual heroic efforts.

- **Scope Creep**

    This is a term used in project management to describe an activity growing beyond what was originally intended. You may become caught up in such added activity, spending too much time on the diversion instead of the critical path of your innovation effort. Evaluate the effects of such a diversion, decide if and how to incorporate it, and communicate to stakeholders either way. Beware of scope creep and being diverted from the critical items of your plan.

- **People Obstacles**

    - **Skills**

        You may discover the team does not have the required skills for a successful project. Consider options like training, hiring, and contracting outside help.

Consider building an ongoing partnership with a staffing firm, to enable a quick response when such needs arise. As Ethel Barrymore once said, "The best time to make friends is before you need them."[3]

- **Turnover**

    Staff turnover or illness could derail a project. Assign a designated backup to key roles like Project Manager, in anticipation of such an occurrence. The designee goes into the project like a backup quarterback prepares for a game - know the game plan, observe as the game unfolds, and be ready to step in if needed.

- **Resistance**

    Resistance may emerge with an individual or individuals on the team, not wanting to follow the plan or continue with their assigned tasks. Share the big picture. Remind them of what the team is trying to achieve, and the importance of their role in that overall effort. This may also be a time to call on your CEO or senior leadership for a pep talk to the team.

- **Shifting Priorities**

    Stakeholders may lose interest along the way, distracted by other priorities. Draw the stakeholders back in with regular and open communications. Ask for stakeholder feedback along the way as well.

- **Technical Obstacles**

    The technology may encounter unexpected issues. Call on the whole team to help overcome such obstacles. Call on in-house or vendor experts to help if needed.

- **Deadlines**

    Impossible deadlines can be demoralizing for the team. Renegotiate the timetable or break the project into chunks. Try to have deliverables with each chunk to demonstrate progress toward the overall goals.

General Approach to Obstacles

Understand the real issue, making sure you are solving the right problem. Analyze approaches, looking for the Russian pencil. Formulate a plan to deal with the obstacle. Keep a positive attitude and visualize success.

> "I never hit a shot, not even in practice, without having a very sharp in-focus picture of it in my head."[4]
>
> Jack Nicklaus
>
> Champion Golfer

Innovation projects will encounter obstacles, often unexpected ones. <u>Navigate</u> around these obstacles to keep the project on track.

Next: CARPE NOVUM - **Offering** encouragement.

Chapter 11: Offer Encouragement

"Champions keep playing until they get it right." [1]

Billie Jean King

Tennis Champion

As an innovation project encounters obstacles or delays, frustration may arise. The initial enthusiasm may wear off as the team faces the work and challenges. There may be increasing doubt and uncertainty about the outcome.

- **Valley of Despair**

    The team may be entering the "valley of despair." [2] This is a term borrowed from the Six Sigma process improvement method, describing the natural phase of a project when frustration sets in:

    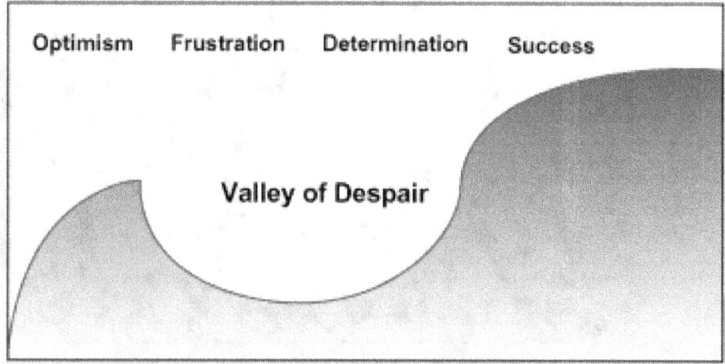

    Initially in an innovation project, your knowledge of this new environment will be diminished. It will take time to gain knowledge of the new. But this feeling of despair and uncertainty will pass. You will climb out of the valley.

    This is a diagram and message I have shared with teams not only for innovation projects, but also acquisition scenarios. These feelings are natural. We will get through this curve, and we will be better for the journey.

- **The Big Picture**

    It is also common for a team member to forget the bigger picture. They may be so caught up in the trees of the effort that they lose sight of the forest. Periodically along the way, take time to remind the team of how their work contributes to the overall success of the project and its strategic value to the organization. This reminder can be a key to ongoing motivation.

- **Value Contributions**

    The old adage of praising in public and criticize in private, comes into play here. Acknowledge the good work, ideas, improvement, and energy of the team or individual. Project status meetings are a good vehicle for this, rather than exclusively waiting until the lessons-learned meeting at the conclusion of the project. Praise should be specific and timely. A thank-you is a very powerful thing.

And with the stress of such a project already, temper your criticism. Still speak up about it, but avoid being too severe. If a mistake was made, for example, ask about how it might be avoided next time. Try to focus on the results ahead.

- **Ownership**

    Micromanagement can lead to the team feeling this is your project, not theirs. Give them opportunities to show their talents and share their ideas. In a team meeting, give everyone an opportunity to speak and contribute, even the quiet and shy ones. The goal is team motivation through the feeling that everyone has ownership in the project.

- **Lead by Example**

    Have a positive attitude; it is contagious. Participate with the team in contributing ideas. Listen intently to the ideas of others. And pitch in. If the team needed to "pull an all-nighter," I felt that I should as well. I would demonstrate that I was not above doing what I asked them to do.

Innovate Like Magic!

Participants in an innovation effort can become disheartened from experiencing dead ends or delays in delivering results. <u>Offer</u> encouragement to keep spirits up and to keep the innovation effort moving forward.

Next: CARPE NOVUM – **Vary** the Plan.

Innovate Like Magic!

Chapter 12: Vary the Plan

"Fifteen years and 5,000 prototypes later, I had a bagless vacuum cleaner." [1]

James Dyson

Perhaps your first attempt will not work as planned. In the case of the Dyson vacuum, James

Innovate Like Magic!

Dyson shared his story of modifications and persistence in the quote above.

- **Do Not Expect Perfection**

    While we all want our plan to be perfect, the reality in the world of innovation projects is our plans are likely to be imperfect. Be prepared to make changes as needed. If your football team is trailing in the fourth quarter by a score of 28-3, maybe it is time to adjust the game plan.

    Be flexible in recognizing the current path is not working. Be bold enough to make a change.

    > "If plan A doesn't work, the alphabet has 25 more letters …." [2]
    >
    > Claire Cook

- **Change can be Good**

    Don't think of change as a negative. It may open your mind to more options and a better outcome. Making changes enables you to still accomplish your goals. Adapting is a positive thing, helping you stay on track.

- **Considerations**

    Clearly identify the change needed. Revisions may be needed to the

    - Goal. Maybe your goal was too aggressive.
    - Timeframe. Maybe the goal could be accomplished with more time.
    - Approach. Maybe the approach chosen is not working out as expected.

    How will the change impact other aspects of the innovation effort? Will the change draw time or resources away from your other objectives? Understand the impact before proceeding.

- **Update Your Plan**

    When you have addressed the needed adjustments and weighed the impact, decide if the change is a go or a no go. If a go, modify your plan document and resume tracking progress.

Innovate Like Magic!

Innovation efforts deal with the unknown, so it is unlikely that yours will be the perfect plan, requiring no modification. <u>Vary</u> the plan as needed. Iterate as needed.

Next: CARPE NOVUM - **Updating** stakeholders.

Chapter 13: Update Stakeholders

"The single biggest problem in communication is the illusion that it has taken place."[1]

George Bernard Shaw

Communicate early and regularly with your team and other stakeholders throughout the innovation project. Put yourself in their shoes and address their concerns. Be open and honest to help retain credibility.

Innovate Like Magic!

Be as transparent as you can, sharing what you know and what you don't. And be aware you may receive questions you do not have all the answers to – yet. Share in a timely fashion, rather than waiting until you have all the answers.

CIOs present to business executives their IT results for the year, IT budgets for next year, and IT plans in alignment with business strategic plans. Here are some tips I've collected in 30+ years of such "executive-friendly" communication. These tips can help you effectively communicate updates on your innovation effort.

- **No Jargon or Wiring Diagrams**

    Avoid technical complexity, or business executives may lose interest quickly. If you must use technical terms, provide short and simple definitions assuming no prior knowledge. Take the time to simplify your message, avoid technical "noise," and your message may be heard.

- **Adapt to the Audience**

    A sales executive may be looking for brevity and a graph to summarize details. The CFO, on the other hand, may want to see more details and numbers, asking many questions. Shape your presentation to the particular audience.

If presenting to both executives or to a group of executives from multiple disciplines, you may need a brief message, while providing details in an attachment.

- **Move the Key Message Upfront**

    It is natural for procedure-oriented IT staff to build the message step-by-step, from assumptions at the beginning through to a logical conclusion at the end. But in reality, the business executive may be called away to respond to a crisis in the middle of your presentation and never hear the conclusion. Or he/she may lose interest by the time the conclusion is reached.

    Move the key message early in the communication. This not only conveys the key message, but may pique interest in the rest of the presentation.

- **Link to Business Direction/Strategy**

    It does not hurt to reiterate the linkage between your innovation effort and the overall direction of the company. Show how this effort supports business strategy.

- **Brevity**

    > "I didn't have time to write a short letter, so I wrote a long one instead."[2]
    >
    > Mark Twain

    Take the time to keep it brief - one page, if possible. This holds the attention of business executives and accomplishes conveying the message before being sidetracked by questions.

    My goal is a one-page executive briefing document that conveys key information:

    - What is the update – good or bad?
    - How does it align with the business?
    - How are we tracking on benefits to the organization?
    - How are we tracking on costs?

- If there are issues or obstacles, what are we planning to do about them going forward?

Address any anticipated concerns or objections. If you have additional supporting documents, numbers or diagrams, attach them to the one page.

- **Use Formatting**

    The structure of the text can enhance readability.

    - **Use Bold Type:** Make key points or phrases jump off the page with the use of bold print.

    - **Bullet Points and Lists:** I tend to list the topics in bold, then list items within those topics, as in the structure of this book. This enables the busy executive to skim the key ideas and dive deeper where interest warrants. Burying the message in long, complex paragraphs does not help convey the message to executives with limited time.

- **Indent:** Like a news format, indent the text or bullet points below a topic. This also helps the busy reader skim the material efficiently. One of my pet peeves is searching through long, rambling text looking for the key points buried within. Invest time in formatting to help the reader.

- **Grammar and Spelling**

    Like having clean grammar and spelling in a resume, it is assumed that an important update will have this adequately covered. It demonstrates an appropriate level of preparation and respect for the audience.

    Years ago, I prepared an excellent IT strategy document, but missed a spelling error on page one. The COO suggested I was "illiterate" and refused to read the document until it was cleaned up. This may have contributed to my sensitivity to this point.

    So take a few minutes to proofread. It would be a good idea to have someone else proofread as well.

Updating stakeholders as you go along is critically important. Keeping everyone in the loop helps sustain buy-in. Communicate status effectively using "executive-friendly" style tips. But most importantly - communicate, communicate, communicate.

Next: CARPE NOVU**M** - **Motivating** for the Future.

Innovate Like Magic!

Chapter 14: Motivate for the Future

"Remember to celebrate milestones as you prepare for the road ahead." [1]

Nelson Mandela

The celebration is the final step. Use this opportunity to acknowledge accomplishments and to motivate stakeholders for the road ahead.

Innovate Like Magic!

Years ago, a colleague shared the following story with me. Struggling with a complex project, her team spent long hours and met the first milestone. She brought in a cake to celebrate the accomplishment — and was reprimanded for bringing in cake without prior approval.

Something was clearly confused in this cake story between ends and means. Going forward, I made it a point to celebrate team and individual accomplishments — and with cake. And I personally served the cake to attendees as a gesture of my gratitude for their efforts.

- **Method**

    Depending on your budget, the celebration can be serving cake as above, or having a potluck, or taking the team out for lunch. The key question to ask is, "What would the team enjoy?" Try to take everyone's needs into account.

    Also the Lessons Learned session can be effectively combined with celebrating the project. Review what went well, what did not go so well, and then ease into the celebration.

- **Invitees**

    Consider inviting stakeholders involved in the innovation effort: the project team, in-house business partners, vendor partners, and senior leadership.

    For the team, it recognizes their performance and encourages participation in future efforts. For senior leadership, this greases the wheels for future innovation requests. Celebration is effective in strengthening relationships with all involved.

- **Thank you**

    This can take various forms: a personal thank-you note, a verbal thank you in private or in public, a small gift as a token of appreciation, or whatever seems appropriate to you. Be genuine and sincere in expressing your gratitude.

- **Remote Stakeholders**

    What do you do with remote stakeholders who cannot celebrate onsite?

Innovate Like Magic!

It is still important to celebrate and recognize their contributors, to help them feel part of the innovation outcome. Try a virtual celebration meeting, using tools like Zoom or Microsoft Teams, for example, to enable everyone to participate.

These events may have a theme, for example: a costume event, or sharing favorite recipes, or playing 2 Truths and a Lie. Be innovative in your celebration!

- **Failures**

    Maybe the innovation effort did not produce the results hoped for. Like your stock portfolio, not every single investment will be a winner. A few big winners can make up for the losses.

    > "Success is 99% failure." [2]
    >
    > Sochiro Honda, Founder of Honda

    o **Be Tolerant of Failure**

    Most organizations, in my experience, are not very good at accepting failure.

Innovate Like Magic!

From an Inc. article by Paul Shoemaker,

> "Most managers pray at the altar of results rather than innovation."[2]

How tolerant are you? Do you hate failures and try to hide them? Do you analyze what happened so you assign blame? Or do you welcome failures and try to learn from them?

- **Celebrate Failures Too**

If you don't celebrate failure, you will discourage future innovation efforts and participation in such efforts. You can kill the spirit of innovation in the organization.

Celebrate failures as these can stimulate new ideas and present new options. Learn from these failures.

> "I haven't failed. I just found 10,000 ways that don't work."[3]
>
> Thomas A. Edison

Innovate Like Magic!

<u>Motivate</u> the team, the executives, and vendor partners for future innovation opportunities. Don't forget to celebrate the effort, even if not successful. Learn and set the stage for future efforts.

Next: We apply the CARPE NOVUM method to three real-world case studies:

- Product
- Process
- Problem Solving

The case studies occurred in three different companies, with three different types of innovation, and each used the CARPE NOVUM method.

Chapter 15: Case Study - Product

An Executive-Friendly Information System

One of my first innovations was the development of an early executive information system (EIS) for the CEO. Here's how the CARPE NOVUM method was used.

- **C – A Culture of Curiosity**

    The Midwestern healthcare organization in this example was young and very open to innovation as a path to growth and competitive advantage. The culture was one of curiosity, finding ways to be improve on products and processes in a mature industry.

- **A – Track Record of Achievement**

    My department was meeting core responsibilities. This plus a few successful projects and my resume, provided enough of a track record for me to be trusted with this innovation opportunity – creating an executive-friendly information system.

- **R – Research Innovation Alternatives**

    Options considered included paper reports, packaged EIS solutions, and a homegrown system.
    - **Paper reports**
        While this option was a sure thing, a well-established format for executive reporting, it would have required

huge volumes of paper to capture all the potential scenarios. This also lacked any wow factor.

- **Packaged EIS Software**

    While this was a relatively-new software category at the time, these solutions were expensive and took 6-12 months to implement. Neither of these characteristics fit with the culture of a fast-moving young company.

- **A Homegrown EIS**

    This was the only path to provide a Wow factor, fast response time, ease of use, quick implementation, and low cost. A homegrown EIS system was the path selected.

- **P – The Innovation Proposal**

    The proposal for this innovation project consisted of the following components:

- **Alignment**

    The project supported a strategic objective – rapid sales growth of this young organization.

- **Benefits**

    The CEO needed to achieve a "single source of truth" for sales figures and to have those numbers available quickly when needed.
    He was frustrated with receiving different answers depending on which executive he asked. And if the data was not readily available, he would encounter delay in having his questions answered. In a fast-paced growth-oriented company, this confusion and delay was unacceptable.

- **Resources**

    I was chosen by the CEO to provide an EIS solution. My small team was available as needed for programming. Advice was available from other departments. The CEO himself was the sponsor of the project. Funding for a prototype was available, but a full rollout of the system would be a decision by the CEO after seeing the prototype.

- **Risks**

  The primary risk for me was my ongoing employment if I failed to deliver a solution for the CEO. For the organization, the risk was time and resources spent on this exploration.

- **Call to Action**

  Approval of the project was made by the CEO.

- **E - Execution of the Project**

  The project was launched immediately. The EIS solution presented these challenges:

  - **Wow Factor**

    Paper reports filled with numbers were the norm, so we opted for colorful maps and bar charts instead, to show sales results. Graphs provide the capability to read the results quickly versus a column of numbers.

From an article on our EIS system, from Best's Review,

> "Information must be presented in a way that is easy to use, read, and interpret."[1]

Because of the volume of possibilities, we chose to deliver the results via PC rather than via huge stacks of reports.

- **Fast Response Time**

    In the early days of PCs, response time for running real-time reports was painfully slow, too slow for executive patience. So we stored screen captures of the resulting graphs to bring up them up instantly.

- **Drill-Down Capability**

    Akin to a drivable PowerPoint presentation, the sales figures were presented in a drill-down fashion -

Innovate Like Magic!

first at an enterprise level, then down to a regional level, and then finally down to a state level.

> "This is a logical, hierarchical view of information. It consists of high-level, aggregate data for the whole corporation, with intermediate levels ... and detail levels …. The executive begins at the top level and is able to drill down to successively lower levels to search for the source of a problem." [1]

If a regional result was not meeting the goal, it was possible to see the results for each state in that region and to quickly see which state was the source of the problem.

- **The Underlying Software**

    While there were EIS packages on the market, the price tag was too high for this midsized company and the response time would have been too slow for executives running real-time reports.

I looked for existing tools that might work, and reused an automated testing tool intended for testing PC software. This tool had screen capture capability and the branching logic needed (e.g., if you press "1", go to this screen). And it was cheap – buy one developer license and deploy the runtime application on any number of PCs.

- **Ease of Use**

    The biggest challenge - how to make this EIS easy enough for an executive who had never before used a PC. To overcome this, the system was designed to be driven by short menus and single keystrokes.

    > "Menus served the purpose well since executives were not comfortable with keyboards: a one-keystroke system met their needs."[1]

No extensive keyboarding was required. A single keystroke would activate the branching logic of the underlying software and bring up the desired bar graph.

- **Results**

    When first demoing the system for the CEO, he gently nudged me aside and took command of the keyboard. From the menu on the screen, he hit a key and the desired sales graph immediately appeared on the PC screen. The EIS system was intuitive enough for him to drive without any training.

    He asked, "To get this graph, should I hit "O" or zero?" My answer, "It is an O, standing for Overview in the menu, but either key will work."

    Having anticipated potential errors, the CEO was sold. He ordered the new EIS system for all the senior leadership team.

    I also shared with the vendor this innovative use of their software. Their response was, "We are not interested, as we are a software testing tool." It reminded me of the Swiss reaction to the digital watch.

Chapter 16: Case Study – Process

Rapid Technology Evaluation Methodology

Now let us apply CARPE NOVUM to another real-world case study - to simplify and accelerate the process of technology evaluation.

- **C – A Culture of Curiosity**

    This Midwestern healthcare organization was more conservative than the one in the previous case study. The primary focus was cost. The cultural philosophy was that cost was the one thing you could control, in good times and in bad times. Innovation was not part of the prevailing culture, unless it was linked to a cost benefit.

- **A – Track Record of Achievement**

    As a relatively new hire, I relied on one successful project at the company and my track record of accomplishment in my resume. This was enough to support my desire to change the current technology selection and acquisition process.

- **R – Research Innovation Alternatives**

    The current technology selection and acquisition process was slow, cumbersome, and delayed achieving the business benefits. I examined the steps of the process:

- **Requesting Technology Information**

    The best tool for soliciting information on technology choices is the Request for Proposal (RFP). This provides a detailed list of specific questions for the vendor to answer about their technology.

    - **The Traditional RFP**

        But traditional RFPs can be exceedingly time-consuming and complex to create. The resulting document could be as much as 300 pages, with hundreds of open-ended questions. This can take as much as 4 months to prepare, per analyst estimates at the time. Plus it took weeks for vendors to respond.

        And some vendors, in seeing the size of the document, decline to respond at all because of the demands on their time. So a possible vendor solution, maybe the best option for the company, was not included in the evaluation.

    - **The RFP-EZ**

        To address these short-comings, I introduced the RFP-EZ, a short form

Innovate Like Magic!

like the U.S. Government's 1040-EZ tax form.

Rather than open-ended answers, the vendor was presented only these five answers:

- Yes. The vendor can do exactly what the question asks.

- No. The vendor does not do what the question asks and has no plans to do so.

- Future. The vendor does not have the capability today, but plans to provide it soon.

- Customization. You have to pay the vendor to customize the product to do that.

- Third Party. The feature is available via a third-party vendor.

A small amount of space is provided for the vendor to elaborate on the answer.

Questions for the vendor would cover

- Business Functionality. Does the solution meet the business need?

- Technical Fit. How well does the solution fit with the existing technology of the organization?

- Support and Training. If a problem with the technology occurs off-hours, will the vendor answer their phone? What training is provided for users and IT staff?

- Speed to Market. How quickly can the vendor deploy the solution (i.e., how quickly can your organization reap the benefits)?

- Cost. Is the cost in-line with the competition, both short- and long-term?

- Vendor Viability. Considering both financial and business model viability, will the vendor be around in a few years to support you and your use of the technology?

Overall the document would be quite short, say 15 pages with the boilerplate material about our company and only 2-3 pages of questions for the vendor.

o **Building a Comparison Matrix**
With the traditional RFP and its open-ended questions, it was time-consuming to review the lengthy responses. And it was often difficult to interpret a particular answer, as the vendors use canned responses that may or may not actually answer the question. Was that a yes or a no? A

Innovate Like Magic!

follow-up call may be required to clarify.

With the RFP-EZ and the five possible answers to a question, it was easy and quick to build a comparison matrix from the responses.

The goal of the comparison matrix was the narrowing of the field to 2 or 3 finalists, to set the stage for competitive contract negotiations. What differentiating factors emerged from the matrix? If all answers to a particular question were "yes," that was not a differentiator. If one said "yes" and another said "no," that became a differentiator.

- **Narrowing the Field**

    Some companies used elaborate scoring systems to determine the leading vendors, one scoring 143 versus another scoring 124 for example. This took time to establish and internally negotiate the weighted scores. And the reason for selecting a vendor was arbitrary, "they scored a

143," which would be hard to explain to senior leadership.

With the RFP-EZ matrix, no internal scoring negotiation was needed. The differentiating factors would narrow the field instantly. Vendor #1 is low-cost, but relatively new to the market. Vendor #2 is higher-cost, but more mature in the market. Vendor #3 does not meet business needs.

- **P – The Innovation Proposal**

    The proposal for this innovation project consisted of the following components:

    - **Alignment**

        The project supported a strategic objective of the organization – cost reduction.

    - **Benefits**

        Speed in technology evaluation meant less time spent by internal resources and quicker realization of benefits.

- **Resources**

    My time was the primary requirement, with others in IT reviewing the work products.

- **Risks**

    The project was low risk. If it didn't work, we would revert to the traditional RFP process.

- **Call to Action**

    Approval of the project was requested of and received from the CIO.

- **E - Execution of the Project**

    The project was launched immediately. A prototype was developed, reviewed internally, and piloted. Results were positive for all stakeholders.

- **Results**

    The entire Rapid Evaluation Methodology (REM) was significantly faster, without sacrificing the quality of the decisions.
    - Technology evaluations now took as little as one month versus 4-6 months.

- Internal staff appreciated the reduced work in preparing and evaluating RFPs.
- Vendors liked the new process because they could respond quickly.
- Vendors no longer refused to respond.

The process held up well over my seven years at the company, producing quality decisions that stood the test of time.

And over 10 years later, this concept emerged in the Federal Government. The Obama administration introduced a similar idea, a simplified form for contractors to bid on government contracts. They also chose the name, "RFP-EZ."

> "RFP-EZ is a new and easy way for companies to learn about and compete for government contracts – in particular, small companies that lack the experience or administrative support generally needed to take full advantage of the Government's Request for Proposals (RFP) process, the means by which many government contract offerings are presented to the business community."[1]

Chapter 17: Case Study – Problem Solving

Bending the Medical Cost Curve

We have reviewed the CARPE NOVUM method as it applies to Product and Process in the previous chapters. Let us apply the method in the next real-world case study - Problem Solving, specifically how to reduce medicals costs by $1 million.

- **C – A Culture of Curiosity**

    The Midwestern healthcare organization in this example had a long history of innovation. It was one of the stated "common values" of the organization. Innovation enabled it to be nimble and often first in its market. Innovations included being an early adopter of an Electronic Medical Records (EMR) system and a patient portal. The portal provided the ability to schedule a clinic appointment, see lab results, securely email clinic staff, and much more. And the innovation continued with the following examples:

    o Check-in kiosks in clinics, similar to those at an airport, allowing patients to check in for an appointment and to collect credit card co-payments.
    o Automated phone calls for outreach, to alert patients to the need for immunizations at appropriate ages or tests based on certain medical conditions.

- o Mobile app, with the ability to access the patient portal via a smartphone.

- **A – Track Record of Achievement**

    Innovation was one component of the holistic IT services at the organization. We did not focus exclusively on innovation and disregard our obligations to provide reliability, low costs, and customer support. The IT department also achieved:

    - o Reliability, with best-in-class EMR uptime over the previous three years of 99.96% or better.
    - o Low costs, with best-in-class IT costs for a company using an EMR system, based on detailed results reported by 45 EMR customers.
    - o Support services, yielding a score of satisfied or very satisfied by 95% of internal IT users surveyed.

    Providing this base of reliable, cost-effective services gave IT the credibility to contribute to the strategic needs of the entire enterprise with this opportunity.

Innovate Like Magic!

- **R – Research Innovation Alternatives**

    The project supported a strategic objective of the organization. Senior Leadership, including the CIO, participated with the Board of Directors in identifying and developing strategic objectives for the year. Medical Cost Savings was one of the four key objectives.

    While there were a number of anecdotal examples of potential cost savings opportunities, data mining was quickly selected as the best approach for finding medical cost savings, without sacrificing healthcare quality. We chose to implement a sweeping investigation of the data, to lead us to the most promising opportunities.

    Why was this approach chosen? It leveraged

    - Our data, collected over the years since EMR implementation as an early adopter. We were positioned to leverage the data we had collected for strategic advantage in developing programs and services to meet the needs of our stakeholders.

- The maturity of the data warehouse. The organization had gone through the pains of data collection and data cleansing, to arrive at the stage of readiness for such a complex, analytical project.
- Our investment in a centralized Data Analytics team in IT, responsible for the data warehouse and for complex analysis of healthcare data.

- **P – The Innovation Proposal**

    The proposal for this innovation project included the following components:

    - **Alignment**

        The project supported a strategic objective of the organization – Medical Cost Savings. The scope consisted of the analysis, identification, and response to cost-savings opportunities.

    - **Benefits**

        The CEO set the aggressive goal of $1 million in savings.

Innovate Like Magic!

- **Resources**
  - IT was chosen as the driver of this strategic objective. Typically IT is an enabler, providing technology support for strategic objectives. A track record of cost savings in the IT budget in recent years provided IT this opportunity to take on the cost challenge at an enterprise level.
  - Staffing. The CIO was named project sponsor of the Medical Cost Savings initiative. The cross-functional project team included the Medical Director, Care Management Manager, Data Analytics Manager, and Data Analytics Analyst.

- **Risks**

  The primary risk was spending time and resources on this exploration, but not finding actionable cost-saving opportunities.

- **Call to Action**

  Approval of the project was requested of and received from Senior Leadership.

- **E - Execution of the Project**

    The project was launched immediately. We attacked the analysis, identification, and response to cost-savings opportunities by

    o Using the Pareto principle to guide us to the leading outliers, based on total cost and also based on the greatest increase in cost trend. As Wikipedia defines it,

    > "The Pareto principle (also known as the 80-20 rule, the law of the vital few, and the principle of factor scarcity) states that, for many events, roughly 80% of the effects come from 20% of the causes."[1]

    o Drilling down to identify the top factors that comprise those events and causes.

    o Identifying potential targets and prioritizing them by charting each on an impact/achievability matrix, where the y axis is impact on the organization and the x axis is probability of achieving the result.

- **Results**

    Seventeen potential targets were identified and prioritized. The leading opportunity was discovered to be Emergency Room (ER) "frequent flyers," patients who visited the ER 6 times or more in a year.

    Note: Results will vary from one organization to the next, based on the leading outliers found. For our organization it was frequent ER visitors.

    - **ER Frequent Flyers**

        How many patients visited the ER more than six times in a year? I guessed maybe 5 or 6, as who would want to spend time in an ER at all, much less multiple times.

        The answer was 98, with associated billed charges of $2.2 million. This was a significant finding and cost-saving opportunity.

A list of the 98 ER frequent flyers was produced for follow-up contact. Findings from this contact included:

- Patients who did not know about Primary Care, a lower-cost alternative to the ER. We educated the person being called, and launched an overall education program for patients to guide them on the use of Primary Care, Urgent Care, and the ER.
- Patients with drug-seeking behavior, visiting Emergency Rooms at various hospitals in the area. They were referred to drug treatment programs.

The project succeeded in "Bending the Cost Curve." As the following graph illustrates, the trend year over year was upward until the year of the ER Frequent Flyer identification and outreach program. Cost avoidance amounted to <u>$500,000 in the first six months</u>. This result was on track to meet our goal all by itself.

Innovate Like Magic!

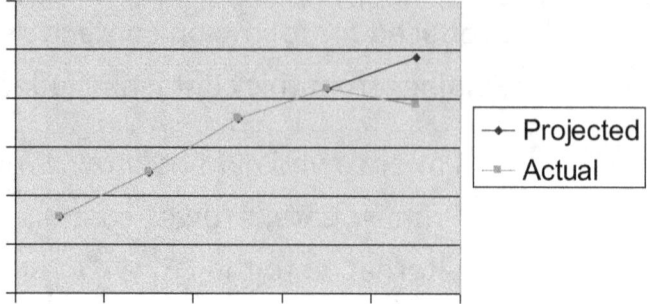

- Two additional target opportunities brought the combined savings to $1.9 million, exceeding the CEO's goal of $1 million. And the savings, from these various target opportunities, were achieved without negatively affecting healthcare quality.

The project won InformationWeek's top national award for IT Innovation in Data Analytics.[2]

Innovate Like Magic!

Our mid-sized company won the innovation competition over major companies like Marriott, Dell, Progressive, FedEx, and Wal-Mart. The win demonstrated that innovation did not require a big company, a big budget, or dropping all other responsibilities.

And <u>3 years</u> after winning the award, this idea continued on in other healthcare organizations. According to Fiercehealthcare.com,

> "Oregon's innovative program to keep 'frequent flyer' patients out of emergency rooms is seeing early signs of success."[3]

Innovate Like Magic!

Chapter 18: Conclusion

Whatever happened to that young boy from the Introduction, who saw his first magic show at age 8?

- o His curiosity led to the study of over one thousand magic magazines, books, and DVDs.

- o His magic performances entertained thousands of people, of all ages, across the United States.

- o Applying the CARPE NOVUM method to the field of magic, he created his own effects and won NBC15's contest for the best original magic trick.

Innovate Like Magic!

And, he begins every magic performance by showing a blank deck of playing cards, a tribute to the trick that first amazed him at age 8 and began his journey of curiosity and innovation. Enjoy it at the link below:

https://youtu.be/fALchzMls-g

Hopefully the ideas and tips in these chapters will help you, as they have helped me, to navigate your innovation journey. Now go innovate – like magic!

In the words of Walt Disney,

> "It's kind of fun to do the impossible."[1]

Notes

Innovations referenced in this book include:

- **Innovations by, or involving, the Author**
    - **Chapter 5**
        - PC install process
        - Attending conferences for free
        - Intradepartmental training
        - "Hostage Exchange" program

    - **Chapter 7**
        - One-page strategic plan
        - Prioritization matrix

    - **Chapter 8**
        - "No member left behind" retention
        - Large Case Management system

    - **Chapter 9**
        - PM-EZ project management

    - **Chapter 15**
        - Executive Information System (EIS)

Innovate Like Magic!

- Chapter 16
  - Rapid Evaluation Methodology (REM)
  - RFP-EZ request for proposal

- Chapter 17
  - Check-in kiosks in clinics
  - Automated phone calls for patient outreach
  - Mobile app for patient portal
  - Bending the cost curve with data analytics

- **Innovations by Others**
  - Chapter 1
    - Drive-through virus testing
    - 3D printers producing face shields
    - Virtual meetings
  - Chapter 5
    - Post-It notes
    - Digital watch
    - Model T Ford
    - NASA pen
    - Dyson vacuum

Introduction

1. J.K. Rowling. Goodreads.com. May 11, 2020.
   <https://www.goodreads.com/quotes/tag/magic>

Chapter 1

1. Merriam-Webster.com, May 11, 2020.
   <https://www.merriam-webster.com/dictionary/innovation>

Chapter 2

1. Amitabh Shukla, What is Innovation? Why Innovation is important? Paggu.com, May 30, 2009.
   <https://www.paggu.com/getting-into-roots/what-is-innovation-why-innovation-is-important>

2. State of Curiosity. Emdgroup.com. May 11, 2020.
   <https://www.emdgroup.com/company/curiosity/status-curiosity-report-en.pdf>

3. Hamza Mudassir, COVID-19 Will Fuel the Next Wave of Innovation. Entrepreneur.com, March 16, 2020.
   <https://www.entrepreneur.com/article/347669>

Chapter 3

1. John Manning, The Disciplined Leader: Keeping the Focus on What Really Matters (Berrett-Koehler Publishers, 2015)

2. Kristi Hedges, How to Drive Innovation in Five Steps. Forbes.com, April 10, 2014. <https://www.forbes.com/sites/work-in-progress/2014/04/10/how-to-drive-innovation-in-five-steps/#63d440343d4b>

3. Galen M. Metz, The Holistic CIO, How to Balance and Overcome Eight Critical Challenges for Today's CIO (Amazon and Kindle, 2017)

Chapter 4

1. Jake Laban, MBA and Jack C. Green, PhD, Communicating Your Strategy. Graziadio Business Review. 2003. <https://gbr.pepperdine.edu/2010/08/communicating-your-strategy>

Chapter 5

1. Dalia Molokhia, The Importance of Being Curious. Harvardbusiness.org. May 24, 2018.

<https://www.harvardbusiness.org/the-importance-of-being-curious>

2. Akila Balasubramaniyan, Spark Innovation with Curiosity. Mahinda.com. July 3, 2019.
<https://www.mahindra.com/news-room/press-release/spark-innovation-with-curiosity>

3. Kathy Taberner & Kirsten Siggins, Institute of Curiosity Survey. May 11, 2020.
<https://instituteofcuriosity.survey.fm/curiosity-test?p=1>

4. Jonathan Wai Ph.D., Seven Ways to Be More Curious. Psychologytoday.com. July 31, 2014.
<https://www.psychologytoday.com/us/blog/finding-the-next-einstein/201407/seven-ways-be-more-curious>

5. Andrew Keshner, The IRS is sending $1,200 stimulus checks to dead people. Marketwatch.com. April 18, 2020.
<https://www.marketwatch.com/story/the-irs-is-sending-1200-stimulus-checks-to-dead-people-and-their-

loved-ones-are-allowed-to-keep-the-money-experts-say-2020-04-16>

6. Stephen R. Covey, Franklincovey.com. May 11, 2020.
    <https://www.franklincovey.com/the-7-habits/habit-5.html>

7. Francesca Gino, Why Curiosity Matters. Hbr.org. September, 2018.
    <https://hbr.org/2018/09/curiosity>

8. Carole Donaldson, The Power of Curiosity in the Workplace. Thetrainingassociates.com. September 17, 2018
    <https://thetrainingassociates.com/blog/power-curiosity-in-workplace>

9. Kristi Hedges, How to Drive Innovation in Five Steps. Forbes.com, April 10, 2014.
    <https://www.forbes.com/sites/work-in-progress/2014/04/10/how-to-drive-innovation-in-five-steps/#63d440343d4b>

10. Galen M. Metz, The Holistic CIO, How to Balance and Overcome Eight Critical Challenges for Today's CIO (Amazon and Kindle, 2017)

11. Philip Chowney, The 7 habits of highly effective people – Habit 6: Synergize. Gbnews.ch. November 29, 2013. <https://www.gbnews.ch/the-7-habits-of-highly-effective-people-habit-6-synergize>

12. Andrew Dickson, How we made the Dyson vacuum cleaner. Theguardian.com. May 24, 2016. <https://www.theguardian.com/culture/2016/may/24/interview-james-dyson-vacuum-cleaner>

Chapter 6

1. Mary K. Pratt, 6 secrets of highly innovative CIOs. CIO.com. January 9, 2018. <https://www.cio.com/article/3245850/6-secrets-of-highly-innovative-cios.html>

2. Marie Kondo, The Life-Changing Magic of Tidying Up: The Japanese Art of Decluttering and Organizing (Ten Speed Press, 2014)

Chapter 7

1. Linus Pauling. Goodreads.com. May 11, 2020.

<https://www.goodreads.com/author/quotes/52938.Linus_Pauling>

2. Michael Treacy and Fred Wiersema, The Discipline of Market Leaders (Basic Books, 2007)

3. Steve Jobs, Goodreads.com. May 11, 2020.
<https://www.goodreads.com/quotes/search?utf8=%E2%9C%93&q=innovation+saying+no+jobs&commit=Search>

Chapter 8

1. Tom Sant, Persuasive Business Proposals: Writing to Win More Customers, Clients, and Contracts (AMACOM, 2003)

2. Geoffrey Moore, Crossing the Chasm, 3rd Edition: Marketing and Selling Disruptive Products to Mainstream Customers (New York: Harper Business, 2014)

Chapter 9

1. Gordon B. Hinckley, Goodreads.com. May 11, 2020.
<https://www.goodreads.com/quotes/24055-you-can-t-plow-a-field-simply-by-turning-it-over>

2. Everything you've ever wanted is on the other side of fear. Virgin.com, November 24, 2017.
   <https://www.virgin.com/richard-branson/everything-youve-ever-wanted-other-side-fear>

3. Galen M. Metz, Secrets of Healthcare IT Revealed! (Amazon and Kindle, 2018)

Chapter 10

1. Robert Burns. Robertburns.org. May 11, 2020.
   <http://www.robertburns.org/works/75.shtml>

2. Karthik Ramchandran, 5 IT Project Management Challenges and How to Overcome Them. Blog.capterra.com. September 18, 2017.
   <https://blog.capterra.com/it-project-management-challenges-and-how-to-overcome-them>

3. Ethel Barrymore. Friendsquotation.com. May 11, 2020.
   <https://www.friendsquotation.com/19580/the-best-time-to-make.php>

4. Jeffrey I. Moore. 7 Proven Ways For Overcoming Obstacles. Everydaypower.com. May 11, 2020. <https://everydaypower.com/ways-for-overcoming-obstacles>

Chapter 11

1. Billie Jean King. Goodreads.com. May 11, 2020. <https://www.goodreads.com/quotes/209337-champions-keep-playing-until-they-get-it-right>

2. ISixSigma.com. May 11, 2020. <https://www.isixsigma.com/new-to-six-sigma/deployment/valley-despair>

Chapter 12

1. Andrew Dickson, How we made the Dyson vacuum cleaner. Theguardian.com. May 24, 2016. <https://www.theguardian.com/culture/2016/may/24/interview-james-dyson-vacuum-cleaner>

2. Claire Cook. Goodreads.com. May 3, 2019. <https://www.goodreads.com/quotes/295704-if-plan-a-doesn-t-work-the-alphabet-has-25-more>

Chapter 13

1. George Bernard Shaw. Goodreads.com. May 11, 2020.
   <https://www.goodreads.com/quotes/tag/communication>

2. Mark Twain. Goodreads.com. May 11, 2020.
   <https://www.goodreads.com/quotes/21422-i-didn-t-have-time-to-write-a-short-letter-so>

Chapter 14

1. Nelson Mandela. Virgin.com. May 11, 2020.
   <https://www.virgin.com/richard-branson/my-top-10-quotes-celebrating>

2. Paul Schoemaker, Why Failure Is the Foundation of Innovation. Inc.com. August 13, 2012.
   <https://www.inc.com/paul-schoemaker/brilliant-failures/why-failure-is-the-foundation-of-innovation.html>

3. Thomas A. Edison. Goodreads.com. May 11, 2020.

<https://www.goodreads.com/quotes/8287-i-have-not-failed-i-ve-just-found-10-000-ways-that>

Chapter 15

1. James Tunis, The Executive's Trusty Assistant. Best's Review. November, 1988.

Chapter 16

1. Karen G. Mills and Todd Park, RFP-EZ Delivers Savings for Taxpayers, New Opportunities for Small Business. Obamawhitehouse.archives.gov. May 15, 2013.
    <https://obamawhitehouse.archives.gov/blog/2013/05/15/rfp-ez-delivers-savings-taxpayers-new-opportunities-small-business>

Chapter 17

1. Vilfredo Pareto. Wikipedia.org. May 11, 2020.
    <https://en.wikipedia.org/wiki/Pareto_principle>

2. Data Mining Reroutes ER 'Frequent Flyers.' InformationWeek, September 13, 2010.

3. Ilene MacDonald, 'Frequent flyer' ER visits drop with coordinated care. Fiercehealthcare.com, July 11, 2013. <https://www.fiercehealthcare.com/healthcare/frequent-flyer-er-visits-drop-coordinated-care>

Chapter 18

1. Stephen Shapiro, 3 Useful Tricks Every Entrepreneur Should Steal From Magicians. Inc.com. April 17, 2018. <https://www.inc.com/stephen-shapiro/how-to-make-impossible-possible-other-useful-tricks-from-magicians.html>

About the Author

Galen M. Metz, FLMI, AIAA, AIM, ACS

Retired after a 40-year career of innovation, Galen is pursuing his retirement dream of being an author, speaker, consultant, and magician.

He is author of

- ***The Holistic CIO, How to Balance and Overcome Eight Critical Challenges for Today's CIO.***
  A Chief Information Officer (CIO) must balance projects, costs, reliability, support, partnerships, staffing, industry comparisons, and innovation. *The Holistic CIO* shares how to address all of these challenges.
- ***Secrets of Healthcare IT Revealed!***
  This book examines each step in the "EHR Continuum," the ongoing workload from a commitment to an Electronic Health Record (EHR) system. It closes with a look into the crystal ball of healthcare IT, including how to lead in uncertain times.

- **Unlock the Secrets of Retirement**
- **Unlock the Secrets of Retirement Workbook**
- **Retirement Ahead – Now What?**

    While much has been written on financial readiness for retirement, these are the first books to provide an easy-to-use, step-by-step, how-to process called CARPE VITAM (Latin for "Seize Life") for planning your dream life in retirement.

Galen has been recognized nationally for his IT leadership and for innovation in technology. This included winning InformationWeek's top national award for innovation in data analytics.

He is also a professional magician, performing at festivals, summer camps, and corporate events. Creating award-winning magical effects, Galen also applies his CARPE NOVUM method to innovation in the field of magic.

Innovate Like Magic!

Innovate Like Magic!

www.ingramcontent.com/pod-product-compliance
Lightning Source LLC
Chambersburg PA
CBHW071401210526
45465CB00001B/204